She Wrote In Scars

Verses Etched in Silence and Strength

Apurva Agarwal

BookLeaf Publishing

India | USA | UK

Made with ❤ on the BookLeaf Publishing Platform
www.bookleafpub.in
www.bookleafpub.com

Dedication

To Divit and Atharv — my little champs, my lifelines.
Even on the toughest days, thinking of you makes the weight feel lighter. You're the quiet strength behind these words and the reason I keep writing.

Preface

She Wrote in Scars: Verses Etched in Silence and Strength is a peek into the quiet corners of the heart — where pain and strength often meet without saying a word. These poems aren't just lines on a page; they're pieces of me, written in the messy moments, the healing ones and everything in between.

This book is especially close to my heart because of two very special boys — my nephews, Divit and Atharv. They're my anchors, my little joys and the purest form of love I know. Their laughter reminds me why we keep going, even when life gets heavy.

Writing has always been my safe space — a way to make sense of the chaos both inside and around me. These poems didn't come rushing out; they took their time, unfolding slowly from quiet thoughts and deep feelings. My hope is that somewhere in these pages, you'll see bits of your own story too — the hard parts, the hopeful parts and everything that makes us human.

This book is a reminder that we all carry scars and through them, we find strength. That silence doesn't mean weakness — sometimes, it's where the real stories live.

Thank you for picking up this book and letting my words sit with you, even just for a little while.

With all my heart,
Apurva Agarwal

Acknowledgements

This book would not have been possible without the unwavering support and love of the most important people in my life.

To the Almighty, whose grace has been my guiding light. In every moment of uncertainty, it is your presence that has provided strength, direction and hope. For the blessings in my life and for the courage to pursue this journey, I am deeply grateful.

To my parents, whose unwavering love and support have been my constant source of strength. Even in moments when we didn't always see eye to eye, you always believed in me and your support—whether in agreement or not—has given me the courage to move forward. Your sacrifices have shaped who I am and I carry your lessons with me in everything I do.

To my close friends, who celebrate my successes more than I do. Your joy for me, your laughter and your genuine happiness are gifts I treasure beyond words. Thank you for always standing by me, for believing in me even when I couldn't believe in myself. Your support has been my anchor and I am eternally grateful for the love and friendship we share.

To all of you, thank you for being the pillars of my strength. This book is as much yours as it is mine.

Turning 30

When I would turn 30
I would have figured it all

When I would turn 30
I would have achieved it all

When I would turn 30
I would have killed it

When I would turn 30
I would be a huge success

Alas, I turned 30 today

Guess what...

I am still trying to figure it out
I don't know what all to achieve
The only thing I have killed is time
I am not a failure but can that be called a success

Age was defined to measure time
It was never meant to be a deadline

What if we achieve something at 31
Something we expected us to achieve by 21

Are we 10 years late
Or are we still in race

Who gets to decide our fate
When it is our decision to make

I won't treat today as any other day
I would pause to think what I achieved along the way

I might not have achieved all that what I wish to
But I did do some pretty good things too

I would like to pat my back for that
While looking forward to what's coming ahead

As I step in my future
There is again a lot to conquer

But since today is not like any other day
I would keep the hustle for another day

Today, I'll sit back and soak it all in
Dance, laugh and maybe go a little mad

Because after all...
Turning 30 is not so bad.

***

Begin

We often regret our past
Complain about the present
And worry about the future

But let's focus on these 24 hours
Let's fill them with joy
Let's embrace gratitude

Wake up each morning
With something beautiful to look forward to
Create, smile and stop procrastinating
Chase that dream, no matter how silly it seems
Start small, but keep moving

Don't do it for anyone else
Do it for yourself

Look at your life
If you're not at the top
It's time to make a change

In the end, remember
You are the result of your own choices.

***

Time Machine

If there were a time machine
I would travel back to the past
I would change so many decisions I made
I would hold on to people and situations I let go
I would avoid every mistake
And excel at everything I tried
I would dive into the things I knew I would love

But now, as I reflect on all these wishes
That perfect life seems so mundane
There would be no ups and downs
How would I know who would pull me up when I fall
How would I know who would comfort me when I cry
How would I know the joy of win after many defeats
How would I know that not having all the answers
Is what truly makes life meaningful

So, I guess I don't need the time machine anymore.
I'm content with the clock ticking forward.

***

Choices

In life, my choices were few and far
Each one demanded its own scar

When troubles came, as they often do
I searched for paths to make it through

Sometimes I had to walk away
Sometimes I stood and chose to stay

But knowing which road I should tread
That's where true wisdom quietly led.

***

The Journey

Confusion, confusion, confusion
Never satisfied with what we have
Uncertain of what will bring us happiness

In this state of confusion
We walk towards a goal
Fearing it might not lead us to joy

But this time, we won't just focus on the goal
We'll appreciate the journey too
We'll make each moment unforgettable

So, even if the end isn't exactly what we hoped for
We'll have gained a priceless experience

An experience that will make us proud
An experience that will bring us smiles
An experience that will strengthen us
An experience that won't haunt us
An experience that will remain as it is

We'll work towards our future,
But we'll make sure to prioritize the present.

***

One Day

I know I couldn't make it
But I'm glad I tried
It's not the same
And it never will be

But it matters to me
It shows my growth
Stepping out of my comfort zone
Facing reality
Facing the world
Facing the truth

And the truth is
There will be times
Many times
When I'll be alone
And all I have to do is
Learn how to live on my own
Then, everything will fall into place

And trust me
It sounds hard
And it is
But not as much as I thought

One day, I'll get there.

***

Today's Promise

Life will have its highs and lows
But my friend, it all still flows
So focus gently on the now
Don't live your life in a somehow

The future stays beyond our sight
It's today that holds the truest light
Smile each moment, laugh awhile
Hold your anger, hearts are fragile

I hope your today is filled with grace,
And success finds you in every chase.

***

One More Moment

We're never truly ready
We always feel we need more time

One more minute
An extra hour
Sometimes even another year
Maybe, in the end, one more life
But we may not get all of that

What we do have is what's in front of us
The now, the real, the present moment
And your response to it
That's what shapes your life

So go on...

Make today your best day
Then try to make tomorrow even better

It might turn out to be your worst
But if you gave it your all
You'll still feel proud

Because in the end, what matters most
Is that every time you fell
You were there to lift yourself up.

***

Then and When

When you're sitting alone, thinking
With the weight of uncertainty clouding your future

Your happy past starts calling
Wrapping you in waves of nostalgia
You scroll through old pictures
Smiling through the tears they bring

But then, your sad past creeps in
Dragging fear back into the room
It reminds you of everything that went wrong
All the choices you wish you hadn't made

Now the joyful past has faded
And the future and pain have teamed up
It's dark all around you
Confusion only grows heavier

Then, unexpectedly
A faint ray of light appears in the distance
You move toward it
And slowly, things begin to clear

It's your present
Standing there with open arms
Radiating hope, free of judgment
Simply waiting to be embraced

So don't make it wait
Get up
Reach out
Hold it close
Because now is the only truth

Everything else—
Is just a story we tell ourselves.

***

The Unknown

Not knowing what's coming
Can feel overwhelming

But even if you knew
Would it really help

People often say
"I wasn't prepared for this"

And maybe, yes
If you saw it coming

You could brace yourself
For the parts that seemed to matter
In that brief window of time

But the things that truly matter
The ones that shift your soul
Those, you're never ready for

We don't grow to control life
We grow to move with it
We don't learn to fix every storm
We learn how to stand

When the winds change
Because no one can stop
The hard moments from finding us
But we can learn
How to keep walking when they do

Yes, we'll pause
To mourn.
To fight.
To rest.
To heal.

And every time
We'll rise a little steadier
A little braver
A little more ourselves

Because it's not over
Not just because it hurts
Not just because it's hard

It's only over,
When we believe it is.

And until then,
We keep going.

***

Hope

Hope is an incredibly powerful word
Its mere presence can help you survive through anything
But when it's absent, it creates a deep void within you

One that nothing else can fill
You'll have to learn to live with that emptiness

When you lose hope in "others"
You lose a relationship.

But when you lose hope in "yourself"
You lose who you are.

***

Heal

It's a cool breeze brushing against my face
I'm feeling a bit cold
It's supposed to be a nice feeling
But my mind is elsewhere

I'm trying hard not to think about what just happened
Or what's been happening these past few weeks
When you place people above yourself
You're bound to get hurt

I knew that
And I did it anyway
Now, I'm hurt
And alone
Wondering where to go
What to do

Still, some part of me believes
Love doesn't really hurt anyone
It's the expectations that do
I'm speechless

You're hurting
And somehow, it feels like it's your fault

What kind of feeling is that?
Definitely not a good one

But I still keep hope alive

That one day,
It will all be okay.

That one day,
This broken heart will heal.

***

The Last Hug

It was departure time
She got up and said goodbye
Walking toward the departure gate
This was the final goodbye now

I hugged her tightly
Though she never really liked hugs
She returned it this time
Tears were on the edge
But I didn't want a crying goodbye
So I turned and headed for the gate

After entering, I looked back
Hoping to see her one last time
But, alas, she was gone

How far we had come
Now it all felt like it was falling apart
I always wanted an elder sister
Tried to find that in her
But relationships don't work that way
I learned that lesson too late

The damage was already done
I was left with only memories
Still, my heart was at peace
I had one perfect last memory

And that was enough to carry me through.
It was our last hug.

***

Goodbye

I am scared of change
Of moving out, letting go
Leaving behind familiar laughs
And watching old roots grow

I wonder what haunts me most
Is it the absence of a few dear souls
Yes, in part
But deeper still, something colder unfolds

What truly frightens me is this
That one day, they'll learn to live without me
Connections once carved into my core
Will fade, just stories in memory

There may be times I flicker in thought
A quiet name in passing breeze
But the space I once held in their lives
Might no longer wait for me.

***

Run Away

Run away to some place

Some place far from reality
Serene and peaceful
Where you rediscover yourself
Where you can hear your own breath

Some place with no clocks, no calendars
Where every moment feels like an adventure
Some place where you are the lead in your story
Where you need nothing to feel whole
Some place where simply being there makes you happy

And when you find that place
Keep it to yourself.

***

Pain

Whenever I'm in pain, I keep moving on
Though nothing changes and the ache goes on
Time begins to blur the edge of the sting
What once felt sharp becomes a softer thing

Then one day, life lands a blow again
A heavy strike, a fresh new strain
But still I walk, though tired and slow
With shoelaces tied, I choose to go

I know there's more pain up ahead
But I won't let it mess with my head
The one thing that refuses to fall
Is my spirit, standing tall through it all

The lesson is simple: embrace the pain,
Never let this life be lived in vain.

***

Debate

"Isn't it lovely to know each other?"
"But aren't we supposed to be rivals?"

"People seem happier with me."
"They live in illusions, until they meet me."

"I thrill them with dreams."
"I ground them in reason."

"I show them what could be."
"I show them what must be."

"They ache when I'm broken."
"That's because they ignored me."

"I'm clearly the best."
"Nope, that's me."

And so,
The heart and the brain
Keep arguing to this very day.

***

The Next Try

I failed 'n' times
Before I finally succeeded on the next try
And every time I triumphed
I found myself wondering
Why did I even fail 'n' times

But whatever the reason
Each attempt held its own meaning
It held its own place in my journey
Because every try mattered
Just as much as the success that followed

And that success?
It's just as fleeting as all the failures before it.

***

Happy Birthday

It is a special day

The day you were born
And with you, many hopes too.

You started growing up
And with that, your dreams too.

Life started happening to you
And with that, the reality checks too.

You met a lot of strangers
And among them, a lot of friends too.

You broke a lot of barriers
And with that, many expectations too.

You realize all this in your mind
And with that, take it to your heart too.

You know it is a special day
But remember, you are special too.

***

Hold On

When things go wrong, as they sometimes will
When the road ahead feels all uphill
When funds run low and debts stack high
And you long to smile but only sigh

Rest if you must, but don't you quit.

***

Precious

Time is precious
Health is precious
Life is precious
Every breath is precious
Relationships are precious
The little moments we enjoy, are precious

Sometimes, everything feels precious
Sometimes, nothing does
Sometimes, precious is just... relative

Go chase what feels precious to you.
It might change.
So should your chasing.

***

www.ingramcontent.com/pod-product-compliance
Lightning Source LLC
LaVergne TN
LVHW010835200726